Presented To:

From:

Date:

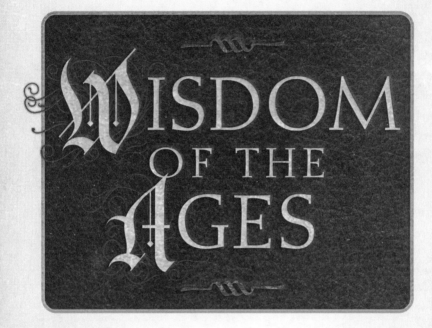

WISDOM OF THE AGES

JIM STOVALL

RIVER OAK PUBLISHING

06 05 04 03   10 9 8 7 6 5 4 3 2 1

Wisdom of the Ages
ISBN 1 –58919-002-5

Copyright © 2003 Jim Stovall

Published by RiverOak Publishing,
An Imprint of Cook Communications Ministries
4050 Lee Vance View
Colorado Springs, Colorado 80918

S ALWAYS, this book and everything I do is
dedicated to my wife, Crystal,
the best writer who lives at my house.

I also wish to acknowledge my parents,
George and Florene Stovall,
who taught me that wisdom does exist
and is worth seeking.

And, finally, I wish to thank
Dorothy Thompson
for turning my words into books.

INTRODUCTION

S SOMEONE WHO SPENDS A GREAT DEAL OF TIME, effort, and energy, turning my thoughts into books, you have paid me the ultimate compliment. You not only admired the attractive cover that my publisher wrapped around my words. But you have decided to invest some of your precious time in the reading of this book. My greatest desire is that your investment of time will be richly rewarded and pay wonderful dividends for the rest of your life.

As a speaker, I have the privilege of standing on stages of arenas and convention centers and sharing my story with many thousands of people. I believe that stories are the greatest teachers of life. In my attempt to impart the Wisdom of the Ages, you and I will journey back centuries and experience a far different time and a different place. Why?

When making transformational decisions in our lives, it is often important to get out of our current time and place—if not physically, at least mentally. This change of environment allows us to examine our lives more objectively and make quality decisions for our future.

You change your life when you change your mind, and you are one decision away from absolutely anything you want.

I will make you the same offer I make to thousands of people who hear me speak from the platform. Any time you are struggling along the path to your destiny and you need someone to believe in you and your dreams, simply pick up the nearest telephone and call me at 918-627-1000. I want you to know that from this day forward, I am privileged to be your partner in success and your ongoing quest for the Wisdom of the Ages.

Respectfully,

JIM STOVALL

CONTENTS

—◈—

1

CHAPTER ONE

THE TRIBUTE

Material possessions will all pass away, but the Wisdom of the Ages will last forever.

NCE UPON A TIME, there was an enchanted kingdom in a land far, far away. The kingdom was ruled by a benevolent and much-loved king. He had led his people through many difficult times, but they had reached a golden age of peace, prosperity, and happiness.

The king summoned all of his wise men together and said, "Now that our land is enjoying a season of prosperity and peace, I wish to leave a permanent legacy of my reign as your ruler."

The king went on to tell his wise men that he would like their best thoughts and ideas as to what he could do to create a fitting tribute to all the people of the kingdom and his reign as their leader. Each of the wise men left the Throne Room determined to come up with the best idea to present to the king, as they all knew that this would be the action taken by the king that would be remembered for generations.

On the appointed day and hour, the wise men reconvened in the Throne Room.

The king said, "I want to hear your suggestions one at a time, so that I might determine what would be a fitting legacy for me to leave in honor of my reign as king."

The first wise man approached the steps leading to the throne, bowed with dignity, and began. "Your highness, since the beginning of recorded history, great rulers have left magnificent feats of architecture as tributes to their greatness. One need only look to the east and think of the great pyramids that have stood for generations and will remain throughout time paying homage to the pharaohs."

The wise man bowed and backed away from the throne.

The king fell silent and was lost in deep thought, then said, "I am pleased with your suggestion as it has much merit. Indeed, a great edifice could stand for thousands of years to proclaim the greatness of our people and my reign as their king."

The second wise man approached the throne and bowed reverently. He said, "Oh, great king, if I may humbly suggest that a gold coin be designed and minted bearing your image and in your honor. This coin could be distributed throughout the kingdom and, carried along the trade routes as if by friendly winds, it would literally be distributed around the world signifying your power and majesty."

The king nodded and smiled. He seemed pleased with this suggestion also. He then beckoned the next wise man to approach. The wise man dutifully bowed and said, "Your highness, may I suggest that a monument of heretofore unknown proportion be erected in your image. Great reflecting pools and immense gardens would surround the statue. People would travel from the four corners of the earth to marvel at its splendor and pay respect and tribute to your greatness."

The king smiled and stated, "Each of these suggestions has been well thought-out and presented. Before I go to deliberate on my final decision, are there any other suggestions?"

After a long pause, the eldest wise man stepped forward. The king smiled and said, "My great and wise advisor, you have been with me from the beginning of my reign to this day, and you have always served me well. What say you in this matter?"

The elderly wise man replied quietly, "Your highness, may I suggest that each of my colleagues has proposed a fitting tribute to your greatness in the traditional sense; however, great buildings, gold coins, and monuments serve as tributes to other rulers from other days. May I humbly offer my suggestion? Something altogether different?

The king nodded in assent.

"The one thing that could pay tribute to your greatness for thousands of years to come would be the proclamation of the Wisdom of the Ages. This would be an opportunity for you, oh Great One, to communicate the greatest secret of the known world to benefit all the human race.

"Buildings and coins and statues will all pass away, but the Wisdom of the Ages would last forever. This would, indeed, be a fitting tribute to the king I humbly serve."

The king fell into deep thought. Finally, he told all of his servants and the wise men to leave him so that he might choose the tribute most fitting to his reign as their king.

CHAPTER TWO

THE SEARCH FOR WISDOM

Wisdom will benefit all people and will forever improve the lives of all humanity.

T CAME TO PASS that for many days the king was not seen throughout the palace. Instead, he deliberated thoughtfully in his private chambers as he wrestled with the question of the permanent tribute to his years on the throne.

The thought of the largest building in the world or even an entire city being erected in his name was compelling. But then, the vision of a beautiful golden coin displaying his likeness seemed more pleasing. And then, again, what leader would not want an ornate monument erected to honor his memory for all time?

Day and night, he struggled with the weight of the question at hand. He paced back and forth throughout his chambers and then walked the length and breadth of the parapet surrounding the castle. The view allowed him to look upon his kingdom from every direction. While he was pleased with all he surveyed, the answer to the question of a fitting tribute eluded him.

After many days, the king once again summoned all of his wise men to the Throne Room. As they entered, the wise men noticed that the king was tired and haggard.

The king spoke in a weary voice. "For many days, I have weighed the decision before me. A great building, a gold coin, or a monument. Each would be a most acceptable and fitting tribute. Yet I continue to ponder this most unique idea of passing on the Wisdom of the Ages as a tribute to our people, our kingdom, and my reign.

"I have not been able to escape from the idea that proclaiming the Wisdom of the Ages would be an ultimate and final tribute. However, what has eluded me these many days is the burning question in my soul."

The king paused dramatically, then looked at each of his wise men in turn. He rose to his feet atop the throne dais and posed the question, "What, after all, is the Wisdom of the Ages?"

The Throne Room fell silent. All present were lost in their own thoughts.

The king broke the silence and proclaimed, "As you are my trusted advisors and wise men, I look collectively to you to articulate the Wisdom of the Ages. Retire now to your chambers, and begin deliberating among yourselves as to the form and nature of the Wisdom of the Ages."

The wise men appeared stunned and forlorn as they shuffled from the Throne Room.

Many days passed, and the king was growing agitated that he had not yet heard from his council of wise men. Shouldn't wise men be able to articulate wisdom?

Finally, he summoned them back to his Throne Room. He said, "For many days, you have been deliberating one question among you. That is, what is the Wisdom of the Ages that I will proclaim as the eternal tribute to my reign as king."

The king looked upon his wise men expectantly. Finally, the eldest and most trusted wise man stepped forward, bowed reverently, and said, "Your Highness, I am most dismayed to inform you that all of your wise men collectively have not been able to agree upon one single aspect of wisdom that you might call the Wisdom of the Ages. While there is certainly much wisdom among us, I know Your Majesty wishes to reduce all wisdom to one single proclamation that will embody the Wisdom of the Ages."

The king sprang to his feet in frustration, his fiery eyes canvassing the assembly of wise men. In a calm but strong voice he stated, "I am very disappointed and somewhat bewildered that all of my advisors—representing the wisdom and experience that I rely on to rule our kingdom—all of you together have been unable to come up with one simple statement of the Wisdom of the Ages."

The king resumed his seat on the throne, gazed upon all of those gathered in the Throne Room, and proclaimed royally, "I, as king, will be forced to decide on this matter, myself, without advice from my wise men."

The king rose and left the Throne Room. He entered his chambers and was not seen again for many days. Once again, he paced the length and breadth of his private quarters and walked around the parapet atop the castle many times, gazing upon the entire kingdom.

Finally, he declared there would be a royal announcement made that very day in the Great Hall of the palace. At the appointed hour, all of the royalty, members of the court, artisans, and nobility were gathered in the ornate and massive Great Hall.

The king entered through a gilded door and moved to the top step. After pausing for several moments, he declared, "My loyal subjects, you have honored me with your dedication and loyalty for many years. Our kingdom has been blessed in recent days. For this reason, I want to leave a legacy of our people and my reign as your king. I have rejected the suggestion of building a huge building, minting a gold coin, or building a massive monument as a tribute. Instead, I have decided to declare and proclaim the Wisdom of the Ages that will stand as a symbol of our collective greatness for all time.

"The Wisdom of the Ages will benefit all people from all lands forever. It will improve the lives of all humanity. However, in order to discover the Wisdom of the Ages sufficient to have an impact upon the lives of all people from all walks of life, we will need to hear from all different types of people declaring their own wisdom. From these declarations, we most certainly will uncover the greatest wisdom of all time. Yea, verily, the Wisdom of the Ages."

As the king paused, the Great Hall was filled with thunderous applause. As the applause died down, the king resumed, "Beginning tomorrow and each day following, in my Throne Room we will hear from one of our citizens declaring his version of the Wisdom of the Ages. By this means, we will certainly establish and be able to proclaim the Wisdom of the Ages to all people for all time as a tribute in perpetuity. So let it be written, and so let it be done."

CHAPTER THREE

THE
MERCHANT

A fair exchange between honorable men

expands all the human race.

 HE NEXT DAY dawned bright and fair. The king rose with a great sense of expectation, as he knew he would begin his quest to discover and proclaim the wisdom of the ages.

At the appointed hour, the king entered his Throne Room, climbed the stairs of the dais, and sat on his throne. The king's court and the nobility, including the wise men, were already assembled throughout the great Throne Room. The king nodded to one of the doormen who opened one of the great doors at the back of the Throne Room and ushered in the first citizen who would share his version of wisdom.

A splendidly dressed elderly man entered the Throne Room and proceeded up the carpeted center aisle. He stopped at the base of the steps that ascended to the throne. He bowed solemnly and waited to be recognized by the king.

After a weighty pause, the king spoke. "All assembled here, pay heed and hear my words. We have gathered together to pursue a tribute to our land, our people, and my reign. This tribute will take the form of a proclamation of the Wisdom of the Ages. We will be hearing from our citizens who will be declaring their own wisdom so that we might discover the ultimate Wisdom of the Ages, which will affect all people for all time."

The king addressed the gentleman before him. "What say you of the Wisdom of the Ages?"

The elderly gentleman bowed again and began. "Your Highness and all nobility assembled here, I humbly ask that you hear my words. I am a merchant. I have been so for many years. As a merchant, I have traveled to all of the greatest markets and ports throughout the civilized world. I have dealt with many people and bargained with them for their prized possessions. I have sold precious goods to the people of our land.

"It has been my experience that people show their true colors when money is involved. The content of a person's character is clearly evident when gold coins are hanging in the balance. My experiences have taught me many lessons and led me to an understanding and a degree of wisdom where people are concerned."

The merchant paused, surveyed all assembled, and addressed the king again. "Your Majesty, the wisdom that has presented itself to me comes predominantly in the form of barter, negotiation, and trading with all types of people. The profound truth I have discovered is that there is no good transaction that is not good for all parties involved. If one party prospers while another suffers, it is a bad trade.

"At the end of a transaction, both parties leave with either money or goods that they did not have before. But the most important thing with which they should leave is a new and solid relationship. Relationship and trust are the basis of all good trades. People far and wide know me and

know my reputation, but above all, they know that my
word is my stock and trade.

"When a merchant treats his customer well, generally that
customer will tell a few close friends of the good experience he has had. But if a merchant treats a customer
poorly or cheats him, that customer will tell everyone he
knows. We live in a world where bad news travels faster
than good news. It takes many years of fair dealing to build
a good reputation, but it takes only a few bad trades to gain
a poor reputation."

The merchant paused, collected his thoughts, and continued with renewed confidence and energy. "When people
deals with me, they enter the transaction with a certain
expectation. Generally, that expectation is based on either
my reputation or what I have promised them. There are no
good or bad deals in and of themselves. They are all judged
on the basis of the initial expectation.

"When people deal with a poor merchant, they will leave
with the feeling that the exchange did not live up to their
expectations. When they deal with a good merchant, they
will leave with the feeling that their expectations were met.
But, when someone deals with a great merchant, the experience will exceed every expectation. That customer becomes
a marketer for that merchant, telling everyone with whom
he has influence of his positive experience.

"Being a merchant—a seller of goods and services—is truly
a high calling, one that honorable young men can aspire to.
We merchants take the best efforts and collected artistry
from craftsmen in the form of goods, and we sell them in
the form of hopes and dreams to hardworking people who
have saved their funds in order to make a transaction.

"We merchants make the wheels of commerce go around. Our goods make people willing to work hard as they aspire to have better lives for themselves and their families. Our gold coins purchase products from tradesmen who give their best effort every day because those efforts are rewarded."

The elderly merchant bowed slightly to the king as he concluded. "Your Majesty, the wisdom I present to you is simple but profound. A fair exchange between honorable men expands all humanity."

The elegantly dressed elderly merchant turned, retraced his original steps along the carpeted aisle, and left the Throne Room through the massive and ornate door. The silence in the Throne Room was broken as the king rose to his feet and addressed the assemblage.

"Indeed today, we have heard wisdom. This wisdom takes a form that I had not considered, but it is, nevertheless, profound. Let us all retire and contemplate the wisdom of the merchant."

4

CHAPTER FOUR

THE SOLDIER

—◆—

If there is nothing worth dying for, there can be

nothing worth living for.

T HE NEXT DAY, the nobility and all of those in the king's court entered the Throne Room with great anticipation. As they took their places, they discussed what they had learned the previous day in the wisdom of the merchant. A number of the king's wise men were sure that the elderly and experienced merchant had certainly expressed the Wisdom of the Ages worthy of the king's tribute.

The Throne Room fell silent as the king entered, mounted the steps of the dais, and sat on his throne. He looked over the assemblage and said, "Certainly you all would agree after yesterday's session that the decision to proclaim the Wisdom of the Ages as a tribute to our people was a good decision. I thought far into the night on the wise words of the merchant and how they might help the human race for years to come.

"Many have denigrated the role of trade and barter as nothing more than greed for greater profits. The merchant showed us that trade is truly about profit, but not just for a few participants. It does lift the quality of life for entire communities and kingdoms.

"Yet, my friends, I do not feel in my heart a level of peace that tells me our quest is finished. And so we shall continue to hear the Wisdom of the Ages as expressed by our most excellent citizenry."

The king nodded to the doorman who opened the door and ushered in the next citizen. A large man walked down the carpeted center aisle wearing full battle armor and carrying a helmet.

He walked with a confidence and a certainty of stride that comes to a man who has seen life and death hanging in the balance on the battlefield. He stopped at the bottom step and saluted the king. The king smiled broadly in recognition.

"All assembled, hear me well," the king stated. "This is a pleasant surprise. Today we will be hearing from one of our land's most honored and decorated soldiers. He has served me well during my reign and led many men into battle who have protected our land. I have often sought his advice when our kingdom was at war and in peril."

The king addressed the soldier directly. "My old friend, I am proud and pleased to have you before me once again in my Throne Room and to hear your words as we seek the Wisdom of the Ages. What say you?"

The soldier spoke boldly and confidently as one who had been in the presence of the king many times. "My commander and king, and all of those gathered in this royal place, my entire life has been spent training to go into battle or in the heat of the battle, itself. That experience has taught me many lessons and given me a degree of wisdom that I bring before you today."

The soldier paused and reflected on his words before he continued. "Our land is enjoying a time of peace, but this was not always the case. For many years, we were at war. Many of my comrades lost their lives in campaigns across the world so that we might enjoy the sweet fruit of peace and prosperity today.

"It is important that the wisdom learned from battle be passed on so that brave soldiers through the ages will not have died in vain.

"War is at the same time the most despicable and glorious pursuit. There is nothing more despicable than those who would take advantage of their strength to oppress others. Might is not always right. On the other hand, there is nothing so glorious as men willing to lay down their lives in a worthy cause.

"I have lost many men who were in my command. They rest in peace knowing that our land is safe and secure for their children and grandchildren. The most profound lesson I have learned from their lives and deaths is that if there is nothing worth dying for, there can be nothing worth living for."

The old soldier paused and let his words sink in. He gazed around the Throne Room and then focused on the king again.

"Throughout recorded history, it has come to pass that old men send young men to battle. As long as it is so, we will have wars to fight. I submit to you that if those who started wars had to fight the wars, the world would be at peace.

"I have risked my life many times and would do so again for this glorious land and the king to whom I have pledged allegiance. However, those in leadership must look upon the declaration and waging of war as the gravest responsibility they face.

"Peace rarely comes and is seldom sustained when people refuse to fight. Peace comes when both sides realize that war is possible and, through fair negotiation, avoid conflict. Peace can only be attained through strength.

"I have seen many men go into battle. There are no heroic men. There are average men faced with heroic tasks. There is nothing that cannot be accomplished when good men are willing to sacrifice everything for a just and worthwhile cause. I would say to my king and to rulers of generations yet to come, 'Look on the face of war as something to be hated and avoided at all costs. Look at the price to be paid in human terms. But, then, when there is no alternative but tyranny and oppression, unleash the might and power of good men battling for a just and glorious cause.'

"In the final analysis, good will always win out over evil, because evil men have nothing to fight for but greed and power. Good men have honor, glory, and the welfare of their children and children's children as a banner to carry into battle.

"Those who do not learn the lessons of war will never know a lasting peace."

The soldier took two steps back, saluted the king, turned, and marched from the Throne Room. A hush fell over all of those assembled.

The king rose solemnly and stated, "We have, indeed, heard and felt wisdom this day. The soldier whose words we consider is worthy to be heard. The very peace and prosperity we enjoy were purchased by him and those like him. May we always honor their memory and heed the words spoken as the wisdom of the soldier."

5

CHAPTER FIVE

THE POET

All poetry does not contain wisdom, but—at

the heart of all wisdom—one will find poetry.

HE THRONE ROOM fell silent as the king entered through his ornate door, climbed the steps of the dais, and settled himself upon his throne. Before he could signal the doorman to usher in the next citizen to set forth his version of the Wisdom of the Ages, a voice called from the gallery where the wise men were seated.

The king called out in annoyance, "Who spoke there? Step forward and be heard."

The youngest of the wise men separated himself from the gallery, walked into the carpeted aisle, and approached the king. He bowed reverently, and the king beckoned him to speak.

"Your Royal Majesty, we have heard the wisdom of the merchant and the wisdom of the soldier. It is very clear that many wise thoughts have been presented to us for consideration. If we continue to hear more each day, I fear we may confuse the issue at hand. Would it not be more prudent for your wise men to deliberate and establish your proclamation of the Wisdom of the Ages now? Certainly the Wisdom of the Ages must have been heard in this room within the last two days."

The king leaned back in his throne and contemplated. Then he addressed the rest of the wise men seated in the gallery.

"Does my council of wise men agree with their young colleague? Have we, indeed, heard enough?"

As the king awaited an answer, an uneasy silence fell over the room. Finally, the eldest and most trusted wise man approached the king. The king nodded to his old friend.

"Your Highness, as always I welcome the opportunity to be heard by you and have you consider my thoughts. My young colleague is arguably the best educated among the wise men; however, at times he suffers from the delusion of many young, well-educated people, thinking that all there is to know is already known. I would submit to you that wisdom is boundless, immense, and eternal. If we are to distill the Wisdom of the Ages into one proclamation for all time, we must hear every bit of thought from as many sources as possible."

The king thanked his old friend and dismissed the youngest wise man with a wave. He rose and surveyed the assemblage.

"Once again, my old friend has served me well. The undertaking of establishing and proclaiming the Wisdom of the Ages is a profound and awesome task. We must, therefore, hear from all our citizens who wish to speak."

The king resumed his place on his throne and signaled to the doorman. A young man entered and slowly walked up the center aisle of the Throne Room. He was dressed in a somewhat casual and haphazard method, particularly for someone approaching the throne of the king. The young man bowed uneasily and began to speak.

"Oh, King, I am a poet, a simple man of words, thoughts, feelings, and ideas. In your search for the Wisdom of the Ages, you must consider the fact that a profound and wise thought is only accepted as such when it can be delivered in a meaningful fashion. All poetry certainly does not contain wisdom, but I believe at the heart of all wisdom, one will find poetry. Throughout recorded history, the poets and the artisans of the word have been those who have laid down the thoughts and feelings of their time.

"Wisdom must stir people's hearts and souls to action, because without action wisdom is nothing more than a theory. It only becomes practical when that wisdom is applied. Therefore, I say that the Wisdom of the Ages is a collection of words and phrases that will stir men's hearts to reach for and achieve their highest ideals. Wisdom is as wisdom does.

"We all have come to know people that we perceive to be wise, but they are wise because of the things they do, not simply by what they say. While a wise man may share his ideas, they will only be accepted if he, himself, is known as one who acts upon them in his daily life."

The poet looked up at the king seeking approval. The king smiled at him and motioned for him to continue. The young poet reached into his tunic and withdrew a worn piece of parchment. He asked, "May I set forth these words for your consideration?"

The king nodded.

The poet glanced down at his parchment. He seemed to grow in stature, and his chest swelled with pride as he began to read.

If I am to dream, let me dream magnificently.
Let me dream grand and lofty thoughts and ideals
That are worthy of me and my best efforts.

If I am to strive, let me strive mightily.
Let me spend myself and my very being
In a quest for that magnificent dream.

And, if I am to stumble, let me stumble but persevere.
Let me learn, grow, and expand myself to join the battle
Renewed for another day and another day and another day.

If I am to win, as I must, let me do so with honor and gratitude.
Honor and gratitude for those people and things that
Made winning possible and so very sweet.

For each of us has been given life as an empty plot of ground.
But on that hallowed ground are the four cornerstones of a great life;
The ability to dream, to strive, to stumble but persevere, and to win.

The common man sees his plot of ground as little more
Than a place to sit and ponder the things that will never be.
But the uncommon man sees his plot of ground as a castle,
A cathedral, a place of learning and healing.

For the uncommon man understands that in these four cornerstones
The Almighty has given us anything—and everything.

The silence in the Throne Room was broken as the king began to applaud. The assemblage joined in the acclamation. The young man held the worn piece of parchment up as a gift for the king. The king climbed down the stairs of the dais and accepted the parchment. The king gave the poet an immense jeweled box that had adorned the table next to the throne.

The poet bowed humbly, held the box, and gazed at it, saying, "Your Highness, it has value beyond compare."

The king was heard to say, "Yes, it does, and I shall treasure it always," as he placed the worn piece of parchment on the table beside the throne.

CHAPTER SIX

THE FARMER

One must invest work and energy for the

expectation of reward in the future.

HE KING SLEPT FITFULLY, and the next morning he paced back and forth in his private chambers. At the outset of his quest for the Wisdom of the Ages, it had been his concern that he might not be able to find enough wisdom. But after just a few days of hearing from citizens of the kingdom, he realized that he would be facing the daunting task of determining what specific wisdom—among all that he had heard—could be deemed the wisdom of the ages.

He called for one of the royal scribes to take down all of the words spoken by the citizens in the coming days.

At the appointed hour, all the wise men and nobility were in their places within the Throne Room. The king, who was seated upon his throne, greeted everyone and signaled the doorman to bring in the next citizen.

A large man entered the Throne Room wearing work clothes. He was neat and clean but, nevertheless, was dressed for labor. His skin was dark brown as someone who spends a great deal of time in the sun during the heat of the day. He was carrying a large wicker basket filled with fresh fruits and vegetables. He seemed uneasy as he walked up the center aisle and approached the throne of the king. He sat his basket on the bottom step of the king's dais and bowed awkwardly.

The king was a bit puzzled by the man standing before him, but he was, nevertheless, determined to hear him out.

"What have you to say to all of those assembled in this place?" the king asked.

The man seemed even more awkward and nervous as he bowed again and began haltingly. "King, I am a simple man, a tiller of the ground and a sower of seeds. I know very little of philosophy or the high-minded things of this world, but being a farmer has taught me many lessons and given me much wisdom that I hope will be useful as you prepare your tribute and proclamation of the Wisdom of the Ages."

The farmer seemed to gain confidence as he continued. "My family and I take great pride in our farm, the work we do, and the crops we grow. Many people in our great land have important tasks and jobs, but we feed them all. Farmers are people of faith. We have little else to guide us. We plow the fields and prepare our land during the spring of the year. We plant seeds in the ground and cultivate our crops through-out the summer. If the rains come and the sun is good, during the fall we have a bountiful crop to harvest.

"At the end of harvest each year, when all the crops have been brought in from the fields, we have a great celebration. This is the time we are thankful for another good year.

"Although the harvest only comes for a brief time each year, each step of the process is vital. Without the plowing, planting, and cultivating, there will be no harvest. Farmers are people who understand that one must invest work and energy for the expectation of reward in the future.

"There are many days after the seed is planted that there is no visible sign of growth in the fields. However, the farmer faithfully goes about his task knowing that the seed is growing within the soil even if it cannot be seen."

The farmer reached into his basket and picked up a potato and an apple. He continued, "These crops teach us many lessons. If we care for and nourish them, they care for and nourish us. But if any step along the way is neglected, there will be no harvest.

"Farmers also learn the valuable lesson that one reaps what one sows. This wisdom is often heard to be said, but is rarely understood by those who do not see it in action as the farmer does. One not only reaps what one sows, but the quality and amount one reaps is directly dependent upon how he sows and cultivates his land.

"For many years, my crops have taught me lessons. They have taught me that even when a farmer works diligently all year, the weather, the insects, and the prevailing market can all greatly affect his rewards. The farmer simply maintains his faith and knowledge that if he continues to take care of his crops, that they will someday again take care of him."

The farmer sat the potato and the apple back in his basket. He looked around the ornate Throne Room, seeming to see it for the first time. He turned back to the king.

"Our kingdom is ruled by you as our leader, and it functions as each individual throughout our land does his or her job to the best of their ability. If one makes leather goods, he may sell his leather to most of the people in the kingdom. If one produces glassware, many throughout the land will want his products. And, if one works with metal, a goodly number of citizens will desire his goods. However, the farmer grows the crops that are consumed by every last person in the kingdom. Those crops sustain our lives and our land.

"Just as the farmer's crops are for everyone, I believe the wisdom of the farmer is intended for every last person no matter who they are or where they're from."

The farmer bowed, leaving his basket of fruits and vegetables before the throne. He then walked back down the aisle and through the ornate door leading out of the Throne Room.

The king walked down the steps of the dais and picked up the basket that the farmer had left. He spoke to all those before him. "Surely we have heard wisdom today. Just as these crops feed and sustain our bodies, the wisdom of the farmer can feed and sustain our minds, spirits, and souls."

7

CHAPTER SEVEN

THE PHYSICIAN

—✐—

Good health is its own reward.

Y THE FIFTH DAY of hearing citizens present their version of the Wisdom of the Ages within the Throne Room, the king, nobility, and wise men had fallen into a pattern that was different than the norm but that seemed comfortable. As the appointed hour approached, everyone would move toward their accustomed places.

But rather than the quiet and somber conversations that had always marked the court mood before the king's entrance, now there was a cacophony of spirited arguments. the nobility would chat amiably among themselves according to their position within the royal stratosphere. But with more zest and bite than they had previously shown in public.

The wise men would be engaged in a heated debate about some nuance of the Wisdom of the Ages or the qualities of the citizens that they had heard from thus far.

Several of the nobles and wise men were petitioning their peers for closure to the debate, arguing on behalf of the wisdom they had heard from the merchant, the soldier, the poet, or the farmer.

Then the king would enter the Throne Room through the massive gilded doors. A hush would fall over the crowd as the king took his place upon the throne.

At the beginning of the fifth session, the king inquired, "Be there any business before this assemblage prior to hearing from our next citizen?"

An elderly and powerful duke rose to his feet and approached the throne. He made a show of bowing before the king, and as the king recognized him with a wave, the duke spoke. "Your Royal Majesty, may I say that it is a tribute to your greatness that we are hearing from all our citizenry regarding the potential Wisdom of the Ages. However, yesterday this body was addressed by a farmer, a mere peasant. We do not even know if he is a landowner. He could be merely an indentured sharecropper."

As the duke paused, the king seemed to be growing agitated. He said, "Do you have a point, or do you just want to hear yourself speak?"

The duke flushed with embarrassment and continued. "Your Majesty, my only concern is for you and your search for the Wisdom of the Ages. I felt, along with some of the nobility, that it would be prudent and expedient for us to hear only from those of noble blood, artisans, or at least those who have qualified themselves in one of the accepted professions. May I say. . . ."

The king thundered, "You may not say. I have heard more of this nonsense than I need to. If the past four days have taught me anything, it is that we need to hear from everyone. The farmer brought us a message of great wisdom, and before me stands a duke I have known for many years whom I have yet to hear utter one syllable of anything remotely approaching what might be called wisdom."

The king glared at the duke and said, "Will there be anything else?"

The duke, his face now white as a sheet, meekly shook his head *no* and resumed his place in the gallery. Nervous and embarrassed coughs could be heard among his peers.

The king addressed those before him again. "Is there anyone else who wishes to be heard?"

The Royal Tomb was never more silent than the Throne Room as the king glared at them all. The king said, "Very well. Hearing no further comment, please bring in our next citizen."

The doorman ushered in a well-dressed, neatly groomed gentleman who was wearing the customary garb of a physician. He bowed before the king and, after being recognized, began to speak.

"Your Highness, I am a physician. I deal with all kinds of people throughout their lives. Often, I am the first person to greet an infant as it enters this world and, many times, I am holding the hand of one of my patients as they leave this world. No matter what else we have as human beings, we have nothing if we don't have our health. Upon his death bed, the wealthiest among us—and even you, oh King—would give everything in your possession for one more day of life."

The physician paused to let his words sink in before he continued. "Health is a matter of cause and effect. Very few people take responsibility for their own health. They ignore this precious gift for far too long and then summon a physician to heal them. People who would not feed their horses or cattle anything less than the best, often abuse and neglect their bodies in a deplorable fashion.

"Many of my colleagues within the medical profession have stooped to pandering to this lack of responsibility taken by many people as it relates to their health. I submit to you that while most physicians treat diseases instead of people, trying to make sick people better, it is a far loftier calling to try to keep well people well. And it is the very pinnacle of the healing profession when a physician undertakes to make well people even better.

"When we, as physicians, live up to our calling, we should all be healers. But not all healers are commonly known as physicians. Those who gather the herbs and compounds from nature that can heal, preserve, and restore health, are definitely healers. Those who teach us to exercise, strengthen, and build our bodies, are also healers. And, beyond a doubt, those who help us heal spiritually and mentally are definitely healers, as all healing is done from the inside out.

"As long as people neglect this marvelous gift of health that they have been given, and as long as physicians treat the disease instead of the person, we will be in a downward spiral as a people.

"We all know many of the rules and habits that result in good health, but too often, people assume that the rules do not apply to them or they can worry about their health later. And then, later never comes.

"There is no one in this great room who does not know enough about how their body works to be more healthy than they are. And there are virtually mountains of information readily available regarding the attainment of vital health.

But it is far too easy to wait until bad habits break down the body and only then seek a cure from a physician.

"We all know that you cannot wait until you are thirsty to start digging the well. You will die of thirst long before you reach the water. Why flirt with disaster and do anything less than the best for this miraculous body you have been given?"

The physician turned to face the wise men and the nobility and then looked back to the king. "We all know that we are going to die someday. Wisdom dictates that we, as a people, learn that there is both a quality and a quantity to life. Good health is its own reward. No matter what other wisdom is available, if one is not alive to hear and understand it, or if one is not healthy enough to pursue it, it simply doesn't matter."

The physician bowed his head before the king, turned, and confidently walked out of the Throne Room.

8

CHAPTER EIGHT

THE JESTER

There is nothing more vital than laughter.

HE KING WAS DEEPLY MOVED by the message delivered by the physician. He thought about it late into the night, and the next morning as he neared the Throne Room, it was still on his mind. As he peered through the gilded door of his special entrance to the Throne Room, he noticed that the nobility and the wise men had already gathered and taken their places.

Perhaps it was his sharp rebuke of the Duke, but today was much quieter. As he entered, a hush replaced the quiet murmur. He sat upon his throne. He scanned the crowd for signs of weariness or boredom. But everyone was eagerly anticipating what words of wisdom this day might bring. When he called for other business, no one stepped forward on this day.

At the signal from the king, the doorman opened the huge door at the back of the Throne Room. Everyone stared at the doorway to discover which of the kingdom's citizens might be coming forth to share their version of the Wisdom of the Ages.

No one entered. But the king sat placidly, and his wise men and nobility had no recourse but to follow suit.

After several awkward moments, the silence grew uneasy. Finally, a growing sound like that of hooves striking the flagstone hall outside the Throne Room grew louder. Then, without warning, a small donkey walked into the Throne Room with a rider, facing backwards, seated in the saddle. The rider was adorned in the most outrageous costume anyone had ever seen.

He began blowing a large horn and ringing a bell as the donkey slowly plodded along the red-carpeted center aisle of the Throne Room. The donkey paused at the bottom step of the dais leading to the throne. His rider slid off the donkey's back and bowed before the king.

The king stared at the spectacle before him in utter amazement. There was not a whisper throughout the immense chamber. Finally, the king's countenance broke into a huge smile, and he began to roar with laughter. The rest of the assemblage followed suit, and some of the noblemen laughed so hard they fell from their seats as they were driven to tears.

Then, as the Throne Room came to order again, the youngest wise man rose and called forth, "Your Majesty, may I be heard?"

The king was still smiling and chuckling as he motioned the young wise man forward. The young wise man bowed and said, "Your Majesty, this is a most serious proceeding. I am appalled that this buffoon would be allowed to appear before this august assemblage."

The young wise man glared as he gestured at the outrageously attired man and donkey standing before the king.

The king looked toward the donkey and citizen before him and inquired, "What might you have to say on this matter?"

He responded, "Your Highness, I agree with the young wise man. This is a most serious matter. Discovering and proclaiming the Wisdom of the Ages for all to hear and know may be the most important undertaking in recorded history. But I would submit to you that nothing is more serious, vital, and important than laughter.

"I have dedicated my life as a jester to making people laugh. I feel it is my duty to lighten their load as they travel through this world."

He patted his donkey on the neck and continued, "Think of how you all felt before my friend and I came into your midst. Then, unexpectedly, you began to experience the precious and wonderful gift of laughter. Laughter has been said to be good medicine. It helps us to gain a perspective on the world that we would not otherwise have.

"As I stand before you with my learned colleague, the donkey, it is hard for you to dwell on the problems and concerns that were weighing you down before we arrived."

The jester turned to the young wise man and continued, "My young friend, I know that you are, indeed, well-educated and learned, but wisdom comes when you can look at and understand all sides of an issue. Sometimes this is not possible until you have had a good laugh. And, in the laughter department, your supply may be seriously depleted."

The king laughed and turned to the young wise man. "I believe that I agree with the jester and his donkey on this matter."

The young wise man bowed slightly and retraced his steps back to his place in the gallery.

The jester continued. "If I were to ask each of you in this room to think of the best times in your life, many of those moments would be adorned with laughter. As royalty and noblemen, you deal with many serious and complex issues. You negotiate treaties and settlements with warring nations. Imagine how much better negotiations would proceed if all debates could begin with a great big laugh."

The jester climbed onto his donkey, once again facing backwards. "I wish you all love and peace and happiness, but above all, I wish you the ability to pause at the most difficult and trying times of life, and simply laugh."

The donkey retreated back down the center aisle of the Throne Room, and as he and the jester exited through the ornate doors, the horn and bell could be heard throughout the Throne Room. Laughter continued to ripple throughout all present.

The king stood and said, "This has been a memorable and wonderful day. May we all remember the wisdom of the jester, and may we all remember to laugh."

CHAPTER NINE

THE TEACHER

Wisdom is eternal, but knowledge changes and

expands moment by moment.

T HE FOLLOWING DAY, all those assembled in the Throne Room were waiting with anticipation to see whom they would hear from next. All eyes were trained on the door at the back of the ornate room as the doorman swung it open wide. The spectacle of the previous day had whetted everyone's appetite, but the citizen who entered the Throne Room and walked down the center aisle was as far removed from the jester on his donkey as one could imagine.

A tall, thin, stoop-shouldered man wearing a scholarly robe approached the bottom step of the dais and bowed solemnly. The king looked down upon him and said, "What have you to say to those assembled to hear of the Wisdom of the Ages?"

The gentleman began to speak. "Your Royal Highness and all those assembled in this great body seeking wisdom, I come before you humbly to submit my own experience as a teacher as the source of my contribution to the Wisdom of the Ages."

He adjusted his glasses and continued, "For over forty years, I have dedicated my life to the teaching, training, and developing of young minds. Many of my students have gone on to be great and wonderful contributors to our society."

The teacher glanced around the Throne Room and with pride said, "Yea, verily, many of my former students are gathered here today and are seated among you. We are all products of the education that we have received from teachers. There is a difference between having an education and having wisdom. All wise men have some education that gives them expertise within a certain realm to understand the world. But not all educated men have wisdom. There are many among us who have great stores of knowledge and no wisdom. Wisdom is the ability to relate and apply learning to the real world.

"Education is a lifelong pursuit. A wise man knows that he is far from obtaining all knowledge. In fact, he understands that the more he learns, the more he needs to learn. At the same time, the foolish man believes that education is a finite process that ends at graduation or when one begins working in his profession.

"All progress made by the human race from the beginning of time is a product of the accumulated body of knowledge. Nothing we see before us today in this room could have been developed from inception to completion by one person within his lifetime. This carpet on which I stand represents the accumulated knowledge of thousands of people over thousands of years. No single man in the wilderness, isolated from other men's learning, could have found the fibers, built the looms, distilled the dyes, and gone through all of the many processes necessary to make this carpet.

"It has been said that a wise man learns from his mistakes. I submit to you that a really wise man learns from other men's mistakes, avoiding the mistake himself.

"It has also been said that when the pupil is ready, the teacher will arrive. I submit to you that the teacher is always there. The variable is the open mind of the pupil.

"Teachers come in many forms. There are those of us trained in the profession who dedicate our very lives to our students. But books can also be teachers as well as other people, nature, and life experiences.

"Learning is available to all of us each day. Wisdom is the process of accepting that learning and implementing it in our daily lives in a meaningful way. The greatest leader does not always have the most knowledge, but ideally he has the most wisdom."

The teacher paused to look at the assemblage. He glanced up at the king and continued. "Your Highness, with all reverence and respect, I submit to you that you are not the man in the kingdom with the most knowledge. Your successful reign as king has demonstrated that you have the most wisdom. You seek counsel from many learned men who have knowledge or experience that you may not have. Your greatness comes from your ability to apply their knowledge, using your wisdom to rule this kingdom and our people.

"The man who seeks knowledge will have knowledge. But unless he understands he must also seek wisdom, his knowledge will not help him and may actually hurt him. The man who seeks wisdom will have both wisdom and knowledge because he understands that in order to master knowledge one must apply wisdom.

"Education is rapidly changing. Beliefs and facts that were held to be true, even a generation ago, are no longer valid. Myths spring up from man's ignorance.

"There was a time in our kingdom when the belief was held that the great sea to our north was the end of the earth. Educated men believed and taught others that if one ventured onto that sea, he would be in danger of falling off into a great void to be attacked by all manner of beasts and dragons.

"Then it was discovered that our land does not end at the great sea, but there is another land on the other side of the sea, and still another one beyond that. One could have mastered that old knowledge and be a slave to it today. Wisdom is eternal, but knowledge changes and expands moment by moment.

"The best of all worlds exists when we can find the old tried-and-true wisdom applied to the newest cutting-edge knowledge. Wisdom is as old as recorded history and remains intact for all time. Knowledge is as new as the next moment and will change even more rapidly in an accelerating fashion on into the future."

The teacher bowed to the king and slowly walked from the Throne Room.

The king stood and spoke. "Indeed, we have heard a great lesson in wisdom delivered by a wonderful and marvelous teacher. May we all remember the lesson we have learned."

10

CHAPTER TEN

THE PARENT

—⁂—

Because parents mold and shape who we are

as individuals, they ultimately determine what

we become as a people.

AS THE SUN CREPT SLOWLY ABOVE THE PEAKS of the far distant mountains, the king was perched high atop the castle on the parapet, surveying his kingdom. His thoughts were of the previous day and the wisdom he had heard from the teacher. He felt thankful that he had been blessed with the knowledge and wisdom necessary to lead his people into a time of peace and prosperity. He prayed that he would continue to be able to be a just, fair, and good leader.

He gazed across the landscape as the villages and hamlets came to life for another day. Far below him on the parade grounds, the knights, horsemen, and soldiers were beginning their daily training exercises. He hoped they would never have to use their skills and weapons of destruction in another real battle.

As he watched the citizens traveling from place to place on the roads and lanes throughout the kingdom on business that only they knew, the king felt pride and honor to be a ruler, yet at the same time the weight and responsibility of leadership.

His valet respectfully beckoned him from the doorway leading from his private chambers onto the parapet. "Your Highness, the hour approaches of the assemblage in the Throne Room. All members of the court, nobility, and wise men have taken their places. They await your presence."

The king smiled and thanked his trusted servant. The king inquired, "How many years have you served as my personal valet?"

The valet was a bit surprised but responded, "Your Majesty, I believe this will be the twenty-seventh year of my service here in the palace."

The king thought of the many years that his servant and friend had been with him.

"I had no idea it had been so long," he said to his servant. "I want to thank you for your outstanding service and valuable friendship."

The humble man bowed slightly and responded, "Your Majesty, may we both be granted another twenty-seven years of service."

The king thought on all these things as he strode into the Throne Room, climbed the steps of the dais, and sat on the throne. He greeted all of those gathered in the gallery and signaled to the doorman to usher in the next citizen.

A young lady stepped through the door and timidly walked up the aisle approaching the throne. While she was trying to appear reverent and dignified, she could not help but keep her eyes from darting about at the marvels of the vast and ornate Throne Room. She knelt before the king and then stood humbly, waiting to be recognized.

The king felt her wonder and fear as he surveyed her face, so he smiled broadly and said, "My lady, thank you for gracing us with your presence this day. We all await your words and your message."

The young lady bowed again and began slowly with a gulp. "Your Majesty, I have no great land nor possessions nor noble title. I have no formal education, and I have not been trained in any of the professions. However, I do believe that my life has brought me a unique and special form of wisdom. I am the mother of five children. They are all healthy, happy, and growing in a way so they can take their places in the world.

"All in the kingdom have been influenced by clergymen, instructors, mentors, friends, and others. But none have influenced us more than our parents, who brought us into the world and who most have molded and shaped who we are and will become.

"Not all parents accept and act on this responsibility. However, all successful children will find a person who serves them in that role."

The mother gazed up at the king for approval. He smiled warmly and nodded for her to continue.

"Being a mother is a balancing act between the head and the heart," she said. "One wishes to pave the way for her children so that they will not experience any of the bumps or ruts that life offers. On the other hand, a parent knows that if a child does not experience some of the small diffi-culties early in life, he or she will not be able to handle large challenges down the road.

"If one is a worker in metal or leather or fabric, he can learn his skill and repeat it in the same fashion day after day. But, as a parent, each child and every situation is different every day.

"Children are a product of their home environment and the way they are raised. However, there is a vast difference among children from their birth. My two oldest sons were born less than three years apart. They were raised in the same home by the same parents. One has become a hunter and swordsman. He is an expert with the bow and can find his way and make his living from the land. His brother is a musician. With little or no training, he is able to conjure the most beautiful music and original melodies from the lyre.

"Our family gave both boys the same values but allowed them each to find his own path. The greatest hope of parents is that their child will be healthy, happy, and the best possible person on whatever path he or she chooses. It is folly to have desires or designs on your child's life beyond that.

"My children will not always be children, but I will always be their mother. The love, concern, and care I feel for them will never die.

"While our society and its policies are shaped by learned men with vast holdings, lofty titles, and significant power, at the heart of everything is a mother's love for her child. No one can have a greater impact on the way we live, grow, and develop as a people."

The mother looked around the Throne Room at all who were gathered to hear her. She continued. "Each of you have my respect, my admiration, and my loyalty for the positions you hold and the duties you perform. But I submit to you that no one will impact the next generation and succeeding generations throughout this kingdom more than a parent.

"May we all solemnly accept that wonderful, blessed responsibility for our children, and may we always be mindful of the fact that there are other children without caring parents who need our love and concern as well. They are our future leaders and hold the keys to the world to come."

11

CHAPTER ELEVEN

THE TRAVELER

True wisdom speaks to the common needs of all people.

HAT NIGHT, the king and all of his wise men were gathered in the great Dining Hall partaking of a sumptuous feast. Many toasts were given between the various courses of the meal. The debate raged on among the wise men as to which bit of wisdom that they had heard might be deemed the Wisdom of the Ages.

Several of the wise men were arguing that it was useless to continue gathering input from more citizens. *Surely they must have heard the Wisdom of the Ages already.*

The youngest and newest wise man rose and petitioned the king. "Your Highness, with the utmost of respect, may I suggest to thee that we now cease this procession of our citizenry and agree to deliberate among ourselves as to the Wisdom of the Ages? What was of interest for a season I fear has now become drudgery."

The king rose to his feet and addressed everyone seated the length of the massive table. "My friends, countrymen, and wise men, I eagerly seek and consider your counsel.

Although we have heard much wisdom to date, in order to be certain that we can proclaim the Wisdom of the Ages, we must be willing to hear from everyone who wishes to speak. Were it something less than my very legacy—our very legacy—to our people, then perhaps we could stop now."

The young wise man looked as if he wanted to say something more to the king. When he looked at the set of the king's expression, however, he thought better of it. With a nod, he took his seat.

The king, a twinkle in his eye and the hint of a smile playing at the corner of his lips, raised his glass and proposed a toast. "To wisdom. May we always seek it and know when we have found it."

Everyone drank, and the festive evening drew to a close.

The next morning, a tall gentleman with a full beard and worn clothes was ushered into the Throne Room. He bowed before the king who beckoned him to speak.

He began slowly. "Your Highness, I have come before you today to speak of the Wisdom of the Ages. I am a traveler. While this land is my home, I have been to many distant kingdoms where I also feel at home. From the time I left my father's house to this day, I have never stayed in one place more than a short season.

"I have seen the far distant mountains to the north with their snowcapped peaks that never melt. I have seen the great oceans and the lands beyond them. I have been across the burning sands of the deserts to the east. During all of my travels, I have experienced much that the world has to offer. In doing so, I believe that I have gained a unique view of wisdom that can only come from many people and peoples."

The traveler gazed around the ornate Throne Room. It was as if he were once again traveling to a foreign land and seeing a great sight.

"It is important to realize that for the Wisdom of the Ages to apply to all people," he continued, "it must fit their language and their culture. While we find gold, silver, and precious stones to be of the highest value, those who call the islands across the sea their home, find little or no value in what we deem so precious. They will readily trade them for things we would consider to be mere trinkets.

"The people of the eastern lands have a great and glorious past of which they are very proud. But their traditions are much different from ours. While they continue to expand the bounds of science, they treasure the thinking of their ancestors.

"In our land, we place great value on youth, beauty, and those who have athletic prowess. In the eastern lands, they revere the elderly as the link to their ancestry and the wisdom of the past.

"Those who spend their lives at sea view the world much differently than those who live upon the land. The sea can never be tamed. The sailor is always subject to its whims. No one can ever control the sea. One can only hope to live with it and learn its secrets.

"The natives of the far distant jungles seem to be very backward to our way of thinking. They seem to be what we would consider uncivilized. When one speaks to them of spiritual or intellectual things, however, their culture and society is shown to run very deep.

"People of the far north deal with ice and snow most of the year round. They are not blessed with crops as we are. But their hunters bring them a variety of game that we, in our land, cannot imagine. Their struggle against the bitter climate has taught them to value teamwork and sharing in much the same way the people of our land pull together when we are attacked by a warring nation. People of the north pull together in their common struggle against the elements."

The traveler reached into his cloak and began to remove items gathered during his journeys, including ivory from the east, jade from the southern regions, as well as strange and unique crystals from the north. He spread the items across the bottom step of the dais leading to the throne.

"Your Highness," he continued, "I leave these treasures from around the world with you as my contribution to your search for the Wisdom of the Ages. May we always remember that wisdom is gained from experience, and the experiences we have had here in our beloved kingdom are much different from those that others around the world have had. For this reason, the Wisdom of the Ages teaches us to look at all people. We must look, not at the things that are different about us, but the things that are the same. The Wisdom of the Ages must be broad enough to speak to the common needs of all people around the world."

The traveler bowed to the king and strode from the Throne Room, leaving a dazzling array of treasures on the step before the king.

The king rose and spoke. "May we ever be mindful of the fact that we live in a blessed land with wonderful people, but there are many other blessed lands with many other wonderful people all around the world. They are our brothers and sisters. May we remember the wisdom of the traveler, and always look beyond the surface differences in people to the heart and mind which are the same in all of creation."

CHAPTER TWELVE

THE TOWN CRIER

Humanity develops and expands from the power of collective knowledge.

HE DEBATE CONTINUED to rage among the wise men regarding the Wisdom of the Ages. The parent. The soldier. The merchant. The traveler. Which person had delivered the greatest wisdom? Many of the wise were sure they knew the answer. Only the eldest and most learned among the wise men remained silent, wishing to hear all of the wisdom before deliberating.

As the king entered the Throne Room, all of those assembled became silent and focused their attention on him. The king greeted everyone, heard some brief business from the gallery, and signaled for the doorman to usher in the next citizen to be heard.

As the ornate door swung open wide, a town crier entered, wearing the traditional garb of his profession and carrying a hand bell. He strode confidently down the center aisle and bowed before the king.

But before the king could grant him permission to speak, the elderly duke rose from his seat in the first row of the gallery. "Your Royal Majesty, may I be heard?" he asked, interrupting the proceedings.

The king appeared annoyed, but beckoned the duke forward. The king inquired, "Pray tell, what have you to say that cannot wait?"

The duke bowed and said, "Your Highness, these proceedings have toiled forward for many days. We have exercised great patience at every turn, but it appears that we are now going to be subjected to hearing from a town crier. What possible wisdom could come from a town crier? Are we to now hear the latest gossip and news of the day? Will that bring us closer to the Wisdom of the Ages?"

The king's face was dark with anger. But he composed himself before replying. Speaking calmly he said, "I submit to you my friend, I don't know what wisdom we are going to hear from the town crier. But that should surprise no one, for because as of yet, we have not been able to hear from him because we have been listening to yet another one of your foolish objections. Your impatience betrays you. I suggest that you find your seat and try to keep your mouth closed unless you feel you have something of significance to discuss. If you do, indeed, feel that you have something important to discuss, something that does not involve your personal aversion to the task at hand, I recommend you consider it carefully before interrupting these proceedings again. Is that clear?"

The duke was deep crimson by the time the king had finished. He muttered something under his breath, bowed briefly, and resumed his seat.

The king addressed the town crier. "Please forgive the interruption. As you know, we are seeking the Wisdom of the Ages in order to pass it on in the form of a proclamation as a tribute to our people."

The king stared at the duke in the first row and resumed. "Some have become overwhelmed and weary by the wisdom we have heard in recent days. Perhaps they have been forced to hear more wisdom in a few days than they have in their previous lifetime. And others, I fear, would not know wisdom if it were to rise up and slap them on the face."

The king motioned for the town crier to begin.

He bowed and spoke. "Your Royal Majesty, as the duke pointed out, as a town crier, I collect and pass on the news of the day from village to village. While the duke, who I do hold in the highest regard, may not place value in that pursuit, I believe the collecting and passing on of news is of great importance and has brought me a measure of wisdom I wish to pass on."

The town crier glanced back at the duke apprehensively, then faced the king and continued. "Since the beginning of time, humanity has developed because of the power of collective knowledge. A person isolated from all other human contact will only know what he experiences himself. But, when we pass information along and learn from one another, it is possible to develop as a society more quickly, because each ensuing generation begins with the previous body of knowledge as a base to work from.

"Many people throughout our kingdom are very familiar with their own lives and careers, but have little or no knowledge of people and activities in the next village, much less across the kingdom. Therefore, without the news from the town crier, they have a very limited perspective.

"Knowing about other people and situations is the beginning of understanding. Understanding is the beginning of tolerance. Tolerance is the beginning of acceptance, and acceptance is the beginning of love.

"Human beings are naturally cautious and fearful of those things and people that they are not familiar with. Having access to the news of other people pulls us all together as one people.

"As a person hears about events that have happened elsewhere, he must not only understand what happened, but begin to understand why it happened and—more importantly—what does it mean to him? If a farmer hears about a drought in a distant land, even though he is not experiencing the drought, he may be reminded to store up reserves in the event that he experiences a drought, himself.

"There is great wisdom that comes from knowing and understanding other people and events. Few among us have the privilege of pursuing that information in person. Those who gather and distribute the news, therefore, make the world a smaller place.

"Ignorance is the reflection of how we are all different. Knowledge is the understanding of how we are much the same. Wisdom is the inner-knowing that we are all one.

"While the passing on of news is critical, the individual who delivers the news must be pure of heart and mind. Ideally, he can only tell others what happened, but must allow them to determine what it means to them. Without that degree of purity, we would simply have an expansion on the town crier's opinion instead of the expansion of knowledge and wisdom.

"Learning about the events of the day will go a long way toward making a person educated and knowledgeable. Applying that education and knowledge to one's current circumstances is the beginning of what we all know as wisdom."

The town crier bowed to the king and walked out of the Throne Room. As the doorman was closing the door behind him, the sound of the crier's bell could still be heard as if at a great distance.

13

CHAPTER THIRTEEN

THE BANKER

—∞—

*Money seldom brings contentment, but those
who spend themselves in service to others will
find true wealth and prosperity.*

HE NEXT DAY dawned bright and sunny across the kingdom. Everyone in the towns and villages went about their daily tasks with eager anticipation. The word was spreading about the search for the Wisdom of the Ages. The town crier was circulating throughout the land, letting everyone know about the proceedings in the Throne Room.

At the appointed hour, the king was seated upon his throne, and all of the wise men and nobility were assembled. The king nodded, and the doorman ushered in an elegantly and expensively dressed elderly gentleman. He was well known to many who were assembled, and no one thought to question his right to speak.

He walked up the aisle and bowed before the king. At the king's signal, he bowed again and began, "Your Royal Highness, I am a banker—a trader in gold and coin. My father before me and my grandfather before him were bankers. I am proud to serve in their tradition."

The banker glanced around the ornate and splendid Throne Room. He seemed to take note of the opulent setting for the first time.

He focused back on the king and continued. "The handling of money can teach us many lessons. The wisdom of these lessons can be applied outside the realm of banking and the simple handling of money.

"Money, in and of itself, is neither good nor bad. Like any other tool, it can be used to build or destroy.

"Thus lessons about money are really lessons about people. Money acts the same way every time. People are always the variable in any transaction. Money can always be trusted to do what it does. Sometimes people cannot be trusted so readily, and other times, they can.

"One of the greatest misconceptions among all humanity is that money will make you happy, and more money will make you even more happy. One need only glance around this Throne Room at the wealth represented here among those of you representing nobility and royalty to know that money does not make you happy.

"While many of you are happy with your lives, I submit to you that you would most probably be happy without your money. Others of you are miserable and think it is because you don't have as much money as others in the royal court.

"If you are not happy now, money will not change your outlook on life. As long as you are pursuing money, you are inflicted with a disease I call *more*. No matter how much wealth someone might acquire, *more* is an elusive and fleeting objective. Instead of having *more* as a goal, human beings should have *contentment* as a goal.

"Those who pursue money rarely ever find enough because money, in and of itself, is not a worthwhile objective. Money is merely the natural result of creating value in the lives of others. The more value you create in the lives of people, the greater your wealth. Those who worry about money never have enough. Those who concern themselves with service to others will enjoy wealth and prosperity.

"Nothing will take the place of money in the tasks that it does. Money is vital for commerce and all parts of our society. But as a focus or a goal, it is shallow at best.

"Money is not the key to wealth. Knowledge, instead, is the key to wealth. If we took all the money in our kingdom and divided it equally among all our citizens, within a few short months or years, the majority of the money would be back in the hands of the people who have it today— because those people understand money and how to make money work for them instead of living a life where they work for money.

"If one enjoys one's work, money is a pleasant by-product of labor. On the other hand, if one does not enjoy one's work, there is not enough money in the world to buy happiness. Who among us would not give every bit of money that they have to save a sick child?

"The things we take for granted, such as family, friends, health, peace, and happiness, have little or nothing to do with the pursuit and accumulation of money."

The banker slowly gazed at the nobility and wise men in turn and then continued with purpose. "More marriages, families, and friendships have been ruined by money than any other cause. Therefore, I feel that the understanding and mastery of money is critical to the discovery of the Wisdom of the Ages.

"There is more suffering that comes from the desire for money than comes from the lack of money. Wealth brings a degree and measure of responsibility. One must make the world a better place for all who live in it, and at the same time, enjoy the fruits of his own labor.

"Food can keep one alive and stop the pain and suffering of hunger. But only when one shares his food with others can he enjoy a banquet.

"Far too many people neglect their family, friends, and neighbors under the guise of working responsibly to earn more money. No amount of money left as an inheritance will take the place of the legacy of love that one can leave who gives time while he is alive instead of money after he is dead.

"People too often know the cost of everything and the value of nothing. Money is a vital and important tool, but the best things in life will always be precious and valuable beyond compare while being free."

The banker bowed reverently to the king who thanked him thoughtfully for his time and wisdom.

14

CHAPTER FOURTEEN

THE HUNTER

Nature revolves in a perfect cycle—and teaches its own innate wisdom.

T HE NEXT MORNING, the king was pacing back and forth across the flagstone floor of his private chambers, talking to his valet. The king was rather agitated as he stated, "It defies all logic. The more information I get, the more confused I seem to become. I thought that the Wisdom of the Ages would be so profound as to stand out above all else. Never would I admit in public, but perhaps the duke and the other impatient grumblers are right."

The king's valet spoke hesitantly. "Your Highness, for these many years, I have served you and watched you lead our people to this time of peace and prosperity. When you have been faced with difficult decisions, you have simply continued to gather information until the right answer presented itself to you. I have confidence that this will be true in your search for the Wisdom of the Ages."

The king nodded slowly. "I hope so," he replied. "This burden weighs heavily on my spirit today."

The king shrugged, broke into a smile, and turned to the valet. "As always, you are much more than a valet," he said. "You are my trusted advisor and dear friend. I am grateful for you."

The valet blushed and bowed slightly, replying, "It has always been and will continue to be my privilege to serve you in every way I can."

The Throne Room was full as the king's court, nobility, and wise men all took their accustomed places. The king entered through the gilded door, climbed the steps of the dais, and paused in front of his throne. He addressed all those assembled.

"After consulting with a trusted advisor . . ."

There was a frantic buzz of conversation among the wise men as each was questioning who was the *trusted advisor.* The king glared at the section of the gallery containing the wise men, and the Throne Room instantly fell silent.

"The search for the Wisdom of the Ages," he continued, "is no different from any other task or decision that has come before this assemblage or me as your king. Once we have gathered enough information, I am confident that the Wisdom of the Ages will be as a priceless diamond buried within the deepest mine. After much effort, it will most certainly reveal itself splendidly to those who seek it diligently."

The king sat upon his throne and signaled to the doorman who ushered in the next citizen to be heard.

A tall, lean, well-muscled gentleman wearing the clothing of a hunter walked down the center aisle. He had a bow and a quiver of arrows upon his back. He had skin tanned the deep color of those who have spent many days out of doors. He paused before the king and bowed somewhat awkwardly.

The king smiled and motioned him to proceed. The guest bowed again more confidently and began to speak.

"O King, I am a hunter. I take my living from the woods and fields throughout our land. My father before me was a hunter, as well as his father before him. Many lessons and much wisdom have been passed down to me. I believe that somewhere within the things I have learned may lie the Wisdom of the Ages that you seek."

The hunter paused, removed his bow and arrows from his back, and set them on the carpeted step. "The wisdom that I bring you this day," he continued, "is not my wisdom or even the wisdom passed down to me from my ancestors. Instead, I bring you wisdom that comes from nature—you might say from the earth itself. The world in its natural state can teach us many lessons.

"All animals, for a time, come under the protection of their parents, but—on the appointed day known only to the mother or father—it is time for that young animal to go into the world on its own. Even though, as a young and less experienced animal, it may be in great danger, the parents know from the instinct passed down from the beginning of time that it is more dangerous not to let their young learn the hard and difficult lessons that life and the wilderness will teach.

"There is a certain pattern and rhythm to nature. It has its own innate wisdom. The geese know the precise day and time to fly south for the winter and north for the summer.

They know how to fly in a formation and protect those birds that may be slower or wounded.

"Nature revolves in a perfect cycle as long as we humans do not interfere. It is important that we have a reverence for nature and learn to respect and honor its ways. The game I hunt is only for the purpose of feeding and clothing the people of our land. I take no joy in killing my prey. I choose to believe that I am merely part of nature's cycle.

"There is a fine line between being the hunter and the hunted. In my world, the hunter can make many mistakes, but the hunted may only make one."

The hunter picked up his bow and arrows, slung them over his shoulder, bowed to the king and court, and strode from the Throne Room.

15

CHAPTER FIFTEEN

THE
HISTORIAN

—m—

A people must know their past before they

can understand their present and move into

their future.

HE NEXT DAY was a dark and dreary morning.

Rain clouds blanketed the kingdom.

As if to outrun the gloom, the king saddled
and mounted his great white charger early that morning.
Galloping across the fields and through the woods surrounding the castle, he was accompanied by four out-
riders who were elite soldiers assigned to the castle for the
purpose of guarding the king.

As he rode, the king contemplated his search for the
Wisdom of the Ages. A steady rain began to fall. He thought
about all of the citizens who had shared their wisdom with
him in the past days.

As the rain pelted down on the king and his magnificent
white steed, he considered what the rain might mean to
the people of the kingdom. He remembered hearing the
wise words from the farmer who had shared about
sowing, reaping, and harvest time. The king knew that the
steady rain would be a blessing to that farmer and all
farmers throughout the land.

The king was also reminded of the hunter whom he had
met just the day before. The king knew that a rain like this
might make it harder for the hunter to track and find his

quarry. The king thought about the patterns and rhythms of nature that the hunter had shared with him as part of his contribution to the Wisdom of the Ages.

The king pointed his large horse back toward the entrance to the castle and eagerly anticipated his session later in the morning. Only a day earlier he felt weary with the enormity of the task. Today he felt a keen excitement at the thought of finding more clues to the Wisdom of the Ages.

At the appointed hour, the king was seated on his throne and signaled to the doorman. He ushered in a very tall, thin, elderly gentleman wearing flowing black robes and carrying two huge leather-bound volumes. The elderly gentleman approached the throne and bowed before the king. He placed the two volumes on the first step of the dais leading up to the throne. The king smiled, seeming to recognize his guest and nodded as a signal of acknowledgement. He beckoned for the robed gentleman to speak.

The gentleman bowed again and began. "Your Highness, I am the Royal Historian. It is my mission to be the keeper of the archives and the Great library of our kingdom. All knowledge is gathered and catalogued in the great library. Since I was a youth when I began as an apprentice—merely carrying books from one place to another—until now when I oversee the entire storehouse of knowledge, I have spent my life among the collected information from all parts of the world."

The historian paused and pointed to the two great leather-bound volumes on the step before him.

"Your Highness, within these pages, and the pages of many thousands of other books, are the collected experience, thoughts, and feelings of people from all walks of life since the beginning of recorded history. If wisdom is—as it has been said—knowledge applied to the real world, the secret to the Wisdom of the Ages must be captured within the walls of the great library of our kingdom.

"Recording the thoughts, emotions, and history of a people is the cornerstone of a civilized society. A people must know their past before they can understand their present and move into their future.

"For example, our history teaches us that our kingdom was founded by a small band of warring nomads who traveled throughout this region gathering their living from the land and from that which they could plunder from weaker people. After several generations, one of your predecessors determined that the people could have a better life if they put down roots and began to plant and till the soil while building permanent homes, schools, and places of worship. That was the beginning of who we are as a people.

"It is impossible to understand you as a leader and us as the citizens of this kingdom unless we know and can learn from our history. Many mistakes were made in our past when we entered into a time of war without good cause or sufficient preparation. Many lives were lost. But if one understands how to use history as a tool, lessons can be learned that can aid in avoiding disasters in the future.

"As one considers history and its role in the Wisdom of the Ages, one must always remember that the past does not always foretell the future. In every experience, one can establish two very different conclusions. Either an experi-ence is a good one that an individual wants to repeat and build upon, or an experience is a bad one that a person wishes to avoid as he moves into the future.

"History is set in stone, but the present represents the quill pen and ink that will write on the page that we will know as the future. The past should never be avoided. It should be embraced, explored, and understood even if it is not pleasant.

"The truth should always be the fundamental pillar of history. Those who are willing to try to rewrite history to make it what they wish it to have been, inevitably fail to learn the lessons that the past can teach them. And all too inevitably, they are doomed to re-create the mistakes of their forefathers.

"As a people, we have not always been perfect, and there are things in our past of which we may not be proud. However, if we can learn from our mistakes and build on our successes, tomorrow will be a brighter day, and we will be remembered as a great people who sought peace, prosperity, and the Wisdom of the Ages."

The historian bowed reverently and looked across the ornate Throne Room at the nobility and wise men assembled. He picked up his two great leather-bound volumes, holding one in each arm and clutching them to his chest. He turned and slowly walked out of the Throne Room.

16

CHAPTER SIXTEEN

THE LABORER

—✺—

A job enjoyed is the beginning of a job mastered.

ONG INTO THE NIGHT, the king rummaged about the aisles of the Great Library of the kingdom. He had been deeply moved by the words of the historian and realized that he had spent far too little time in this vast storehouse of knowledge.

The king spent many hours poring over the ancient volumes of recorded history about his ancestors. He knew he had become king because his father and grandfather had been kings, but as he explored the many rulers in his lineage, he felt a deeper responsibility for his position of leadership than he had ever felt before.

He realized that his responsibility extended not only to the present citizens of the kingdom, but his responsibility extended also to the past leaders and citizens so that he might carry on and build upon their legacy.

Finally, just before dawn, the king grew too tired to read anymore and summoned the historian to let him know that he would be leaving the library.

The historian bowed reverently and said, "Your Majesty, it is always a privilege to have you partake of the knowledge within the Great Library. Before we leave, however, I must replace the volumes that you have been reading upon their respective shelves."

As the king stood by and looked on, the historian reverently picked up each of the volumes and lovingly replaced them on the shelves.

As he walked back to his private quarters, the king thought about how the historian's love of knowledge was reflected tangibly in his care and reverence for the volumes, themselves.

The king lay down and fell into a deep and dreamless sleep. Little more than an hour later, he rose, feeling remarkably refreshed after such a short night of sleep. He took his breakfast on the upper parapet, surveying the land below him. The sun shone brightly on the towns, fields, and villages of the kingdom.

Yesterday he had been so keen for the task ahead. On this day, more than ever, he felt the responsibility of discovering and revealing the Wisdom of the Ages weighing heavily on his soul. *Maybe I'm not as rested as I had hoped,* he thought. He reflected on a man his age spending the night poring over ancient volumes of history and what a sight that must have been. A small smile played at the corners of his mouth and he did, indeed, feel better and perhaps up for the task at hand.

After his valet informed him that it was time for the court to assemble, the king rose from his breakfast table, walked through the castle, and entered the Throne Room. He mounted the steps of the dais and took his place on the throne. The ornate room fell silent as the king gazed out on the nobility and assembled wise men.

He signaled to the doorman who ushered in a large, muscular young man wearing very rough work clothes. The young man seemed dazzled by his surroundings and hesitantly approached the king. He stopped several paces from the bottom step of the dais leading to the throne.

The king smiled and beckoned the young man to approach. The young man moved to the bottom step and bowed awkwardly. The king motioned for him to proceed.

"Your Royal Highness, I have no great title, nor immense wealth, nor vast education. I am but a humble laborer."

The young man seemed to falter in his speech. The king smiled warmly and nodded encouragingly for the young man to continue.

"The wisdom I know is the things that I have learned from my strong back and my skilled hands. I am proud to say that I had a small part in fitting the stones that are in these magnificent walls you see surrounding you."

The young man pointed to each of the walls and seemed to gather confidence as he continued. "There is no job insignificant enough that it should not be done with pride, skill, and all the effort that one possesses.

"Our society is a compilation of everyone doing their respective jobs to the best of their ability. This is only possible when people pursue their passion. A job enjoyed is the beginning of a job mastered.

"Some laborers only work in order to put in enough hours to receive their coins at the end of the day. While I have exactly the same job, it is one I relish and enjoy as a privilege. They put stones atop one another in exchange for coins, and they see little else from their efforts. I, on the other hand, see in my mind the great castles and cathedrals throughout our land. My labors bring those wonderful monuments from my mind into the reality that we all know and can enjoy.

"A poorly fitted stone may result in the laborer receiving a few coins at the end of the day. But a well-fitted stone is a work of art that will stand for a thousand years as a monument to the love and care and passion of the laborer.

"I have also learned that while I can apply my skill to the work with the stones, I cannot create a magnificent structure like this Throne Room by myself. The carpenters, stained-glass artists, and metalworkers all must do their part in order for us to be able to enjoy this wonderful Throne Room.

"Just as each stone on every level of a wall is critical to the integrity of that wall, each laborer from all the crafts must perform his task well in order to have a successful project. If one stone in this wall before you . . ."

He walked toward the massive wall at the side of the Throne Room and touched one of the stones.

". . . does not fit perfectly, it will become the weak spot in the entire structure. Over the years, water will seep in and begin to erode and affect the integrity of the entire structure. This wall represents my best labor for many days and weeks. If I had but one bad day and allowed that to reflect upon my work, the entire wall would be affected, not just the stones I set poorly.

"I have learned some portion of wisdom from my years of labor. Our lives and relationships are much like the stone wall. One bad day, poor performance, or unkind word can adversely affect many years of good relationships, hard work, and positive reputation.

"When laborers work together with that attitude, it becomes a very positive environment as no one wants to disappoint their fellow workers. I know that, while the metalworkers and carpenters were setting that magnificent door in the back of the Throne Room, they looked for many days upon my stonework and me as I labored. They knew that no matter how good and even my stonework, that if their door was not set properly, the Throne Room would not be of the magnificent quality you see before you today.

"I don't know much about what learned and scholarly men do as they go about their daily business, but I do know that if we all give our maximum effort to that task for which we feel power and passion, the world will be a better place to live."

The laborer bowed humbly and walked from the Throne Room.

The king sat upon his throne and gazed upon the wall of massive stones to his left. He realized that he had never seen the wall quite in this light before, and he knew that he would never overlook a job well done by a laborer ever again.

17

CHAPTER SEVENTEEN

THE SCIENTIST

*Science and the quest for knowledge are not a
destination but a lifelong, never-ending journey.*

HAT NIGHT, the king watched the golden ball of fire that was the sun slide below the western mountains. He realized that the crown jewels were nothing compared to the light show that graced the western sky each evening.

As he stood high atop the parapet above the castle, he could not help but notice the marvelous craftsmanship that had gone into the flagstone deck below his feet. After hearing the wisdom of the laborer earlier that same day, he knew that he could never again look upon another man's work and see it as common if it was a job well done.

As the glow in the west continued to fade, he contemplated the overwhelming task of discovering and proclaiming the Wisdom of the Ages. Each day, there was more and more wisdom to consider as the various citizens from all walks of life shared their own experiences of life and learning.

Long after nightfall had enveloped the kingdom, the king finally retired to his private chambers. He slept fitfully, feeling anew the pressure of the obligation weighing heavily on his mind. He awoke early the next morning and had his valet serve breakfast within his chambers. He needed more time to prepare himself emotionally and mentally for the day.

He could not remember if the days of waging war had taxed his soul as much as this ultimate search for wisdom now demanded from him.

As the king entered the Throne Room through the ornate gilded door, he was once again struck by the incredible workmanship and loving labor that had gone into the appointments throughout the Throne Room. As he climbed the steps of the dais and sat upon his throne, he observed that the nobility and wise men were, likewise, observing the labor and workmanship that had gone into the walls and fixtures around them. The king sat for a moment and realized that this gathering of shared wisdom was affecting them all. Even his nettlesome friend, the proud and haughty duke, looked a little more humble and reflective this morning. He smiled to himself as he thought, *the search for wisdom does have its rewards.*

Finally, he signaled to the doorman at the back of the great room, who ushered in a white-haired, somewhat-disheveled gentleman who walked down the center aisle and bowed to the king.

The king looked at the citizen before him. He thought that the man was not as much unkempt as he was someone who simply who did not concern himself with his attire or outward appearance. The king beckoned him to speak, and the white-haired gentleman began.

"Your Royal Highness and all those assembled in this great place seeking the Wisdom of the Ages, it is my privilege and distinct honor to come before you this day to be heard. I am a scientist—an explorer of nature and all the elements of this world that we have been given. My studies and experiments have given me what I believe to be a degree of wisdom that I hope will be a key that unlocks the Wisdom of the Ages."

The scientist glanced up at the king, seeming to seek approval. The king smiled warmly and nodded for the scientist to continue.

"Your Majesty, the scientific world around us teaches us many lessons. One obvious observation is that the body of accumulated knowledge continues to grow and accelerate. With that, there is a certain arrogance that develops among learned men. It comes as they compare the many things they know about the world to what the scientists and educators from the decades and centuries before them knew.

"I know much more today than did the professors and scientists who taught me. Not because I am more intelligent or more learned, but because the scientific world has continued to advance. I can see a more distant horizon of the scientific world than could the giants who went before me. This is only because I stand as a dwarf on their shoulders as I look forward.

"The work they had accumulated at the end of their lives is the place I began, and in much the same way, young people today will take my work and advance it further than I can dream.

"Yes, a hundred years from now, there will be a young student somewhere whose knowledge and understanding will be at a level I cannot even imagine. His arrogance may cause him to look upon my work and consider my colleagues and me to be very ignorant and backward.

"Those who have not studied the scientific methodology through the world around them can easily come under the false impression that everything that there is to know is already known. This is utter folly."

The scientist seemed to change directions in his mind. He looked into the gallery and addressed the noblemen and wise men as if they were a class and he was their professor.

"One must realize that the world around us works on the basis of a magnificent set of unchanging and unalterable principles. Water freezes the same way at the same point every time. When you think you have located an inconsistency in nature, it is merely a new principle.

"For example, it has been known for years that all water will freeze at a certain temperature. The first scientist who noticed a frozen river leading into the sea, which was not frozen, may have thought he discovered an inconsistency as the water in the river was frozen solid and the sea was not. That scientist did not discover an inconsistency, but instead, a new consistent principle. That is, fresh water freezes at one temperature and salt water another.

"Science and the quest for knowledge are not a destination but a lifelong, never-ending journey. The more one discovers and knows, the more one realizes that there remains more yet to be known. This has ever been the case and will continue to be so.

"Many of my misguided colleagues forget that the universal rules and laws of science apply to us all whether or not we understand them or agree with them. Gravity works every time. Any of us from the king to the lowliest peasant who would climb to the highest point of this castle and step off into space would surely die.

"The fact that birds do not seem to be affected by gravity does not mean gravity is not consistent. It means that there are other aerodynamic laws of science to be studied and learned.

"Science must always progress, but it must be harnessed as the servant of man. Science and development, unbridled, can lead to mass destruction. Knowledge, itself, is never harmful, but the improper utilization of knowledge can be devastating.

"May we all continue to grow and develop and accept the responsibility that goes along with the dawning of the new day of science."

The scientist bowed once again to the king and those assembled in the gallery. He slowly walked from the Throne Room.

The king fell silent as he and everyone within the great Throne Room contemplated that which they had heard.

18

CHAPTER EIGHTEEN

THE JUDGE

The ability to understand and be understood

is at the heart of all agreements and

human interaction.

HE NEXT MORNING, the king was up and dressed before dawn. He walked out of the castle and wandered among the fields and woods in the vicinity. His guards followed him. He had made it clear that he wished to be alone to think, so they remained at a discreet and respectful distance.

The king saw a bird perched on a branch of a large tree. As he approached, the bird flew from the branch as a leaf fell. He remembered the words of the scientist. Both the leaf and the bird are affected by gravity, but there are other principles in place. The king realized that there are life principles and wisdom pertaining to every situation, but one must apply the right principles, or he will arrive at the wrong conclusion.

The king pondered all of the accumulated knowledge of science, and—for the first time in his life—was able to see that entire body of knowledge as a small speck on the horizon of human potential.

The king continued to walk through the woods and fields until the day had fully dawned. He startled several early travelers as they recognized him and were surprised to see the king walking a village path early in the morning.

The king greeted everyone he met warmly. His search for the Wisdom of the Ages was daily teaching him that there is wisdom and greatness in everyone. While royalty may hold a recognized and honored title, wisdom is even more valuable, though often hidden within otherwise mundane packages.

Eventually, the palace guards approached the king and respectfully reminded him of his morning session in the Throne Room. The king was somewhat disappointed, as he was immensely enjoying this early morning wandering throughout nature. Finally, the king turned toward the castle and began contemplating the day before him.

Once again upon his throne, the king gave a signal. The doorman ushered in a distinguished-looking gentleman wearing splendid judicial robes with full regalia. The gentle-man confidently strode to the base of the dais, bowed before the king, and at the king's nod—began to speak.

"Your Royal Majesty, I am proud to serve you and the people of this kingdom as a judge of the law. For it is the law that gives us a civilized society. As a judge, I have had every type of person in every type of situation appear before me. I have had to weigh and consider many aspects of life and have, hopefully, in so doing, obtained a measure of wisdom that I wish to present to you.

"Our society is defined by the laws that all are obliged to adhere to. Without these accepted laws, anarchy would reign among us. The greatness of a society can be deter-mined by how the laws are applied to all the citizens, from the highest to the lowest. It is a short distance from someone being above the law to everyone living outside the law."

The judge looked directly at the king as he continued to speak.

"Your Highness, one of the tributes of your greatness as a leader is the fact that you realize that the laws of the land must apply to you as equally as to all of the other citizens. It is not enough to give lip service to the law. We must obey it and understand that the law exists not to deprive us of freedom, but to deliver us unto freedom. Men can only live free lives when their expression of freedom does not trample on their fellow citizens' freedom.

"The law is imperfect, yes, but as long as evil resides in the hearts and minds of a few of us, the law must guide all of us. In a perfect world, people would not steal because they recognize that it is the wrong thing to do, and it diminishes their own value. However, there are some men who feel that the gold to be gained in thievery is more precious than the humanity to be lost, and they would steal if the law and punishment did not prevent it.

"Most of us go about our daily lives and treat others and their property with respect because it is the way that we, ourselves, wish to be treated. However, for the few among us who are not respectful of these things, the law must stand as our model.

"There should be as few laws as possible while still maintaining order within society. Too many laws and restrictions limit the very freedom that the law exists to protect.

"Man's law will always be developing and changing as our societal norms and needs develop and change. Scientific development, the growth of trade and interaction with other cultures, a larger and more crowded population—all these things will necessitate the need for different and unique laws, but we must always remember that human rights and freedom remain paramount.

"As a judge, I have had many people stand before me to hear their grievances. Almost all of these disputes could have been resolved outside of my courtroom with far less cost and damage to relationships if those involved would have maintained a respect for one another's rights and simply been willing to talk civilly among themselves.

"The ability to understand and be understood is at the heart of all agreements and human interaction. Hearing is not necessarily understanding. Understanding is not necessarily accepting. Hearing is a function of the ear. Understanding is a function of the brain. But acceptance is a function of the heart. If we can all live and interact on the level of acceptance, laws will rarely come into play."

The judge bowed reverently to the king. The king thanked him for his profound words. The judge nodded to several of his friends among the nobility as he strode from the Throne Room.

All of those gathered sat and thought about how they could live and learn within the spirit of the law. None pondered harder than the king.

19

CHAPTER NINETEEN

THE ELDER

—⁓—

Life is the greatest teacher and the ultimate

purveyor of wisdom.

THE NEXT MORNING, the king presided over his regular council meeting, which dealt with all of the business of the kingdom. His advisors and the nobility were present along with the wise men. He listened to a number of issues and debates dealing with foreign trade, treaties, and domestic matters from across the various towns and villages comprising the kingdom.

The king tired of these mundane duties, but he knew they were important and must be dispatched. His mind kept wandering back to the search for the Wisdom of the Ages. He felt the mixed emotions of relief—because he knew that there was only one citizen left who would be coming before him to present the wisdom he had found—and sadness, for he knew that his life was greatly enriched through the search.

Near the end of the scheduled council session, one of the advisors rose, bowed, and addressed the king.

"Your Highness, we have a matter of growing importance to bring to your attention. It seems that our citizens from all across the land are expressing a keen interest in your pending proclamation of the Wisdom of the Ages. Many debates are raging throughout the towns and villages as to what the Wisdom of the Ages will comprise.

"All of your subjects are anxiously awaiting and eagerly anticipating your proclamation. As there is only one last scheduled session in the Throne Room regarding the Wisdom of the Ages, we—your advisors and wise men— feel that you need to set a date when you will be making your proclamation of the Wisdom of the Ages. This will give your citizens something to look forward to and set their minds at peace."

The king thought for a moment and then responded, "We will be hearing from our last citizen today regarding the Wisdom of the Ages, so tomorrow will be the day that I set forth my tribute to our people and my reign as their king as I proclaim for all time the Wisdom of the Ages."

All of those assembled in the council room applauded the king's announcement. The king gazed boldly and calmly at his assembly, but on the inside his emotions roiled and he felt a twinge of fear. He realized more than ever that everyone in the kingdom would be looking to him to discover, define, and proclaim the Wisdom of the Ages. *A monument or a coin would have been so much easier* he thought ruefully.

Although he had heard many great revelations and much wisdom from the citizenry over the past several weeks, there was no clearly defined universal wisdom that stood apart so dramatically that he felt he could proclaim as the Wisdom of the Ages. At least not yet, for there was to be another presentation today.

At the appointed hour of the last session within the Throne Room, the king entered through his personal ornately gilded door, climbed the steps of the dais, and sat upon his throne. He could feel the tension in the room as the culmination of the search for the Wisdom of the Ages was drawing to a close.

The king sat in silence for a moment and then, resolved to press ahead, signaled for the doorman to usher in the last citizen to be heard. As the doorman swung open the door, a very elderly, stooped-shouldered man shuffled into the Throne Room and began making his way slowly down the aisle to the throne. He wore gray robes and had long, flowing, snow-white hair and beard.

At the base of the steps leading to the throne, the elderly man nodded more than bowed and stood, waiting to be recognized. The king motioned for the man to speak, and he began.

"Your Royal Majesty, I have been a loyal subject of this kingdom longer than anyone else alive today."

Everyone in the Throne Room leaned forward to hear the elderly gentleman, as his voice was soft and raspy.

"Throughout my century of life," he continued, "I have learned many lessons and gained much wisdom that I feel should be included within the Wisdom of the Ages. Life contains many mysteries. Many of them can be solved only to reveal more elaborate and confusing mysteries.

"As a young man, I felt I knew and understood everything. The world was simple, and solutions were easy to come by. As the years passed, I came to realize that the world is not simple, and real truth is very rare and precious.

"We live in a society that, more and more, reveres youth as well as new things and new ideas. While I would be the first to admit that youth has its benefits, wisdom can only be obtained through experience, either one's own experiences, or ones shared from another.

"Difficulties in life can only be avoided by utilizing the good judgment that comes from wisdom. Wisdom and good judgment can only be gained from experiencing life's difficulties.

"I believe that a society can be judged on the basis of how it treats its elder citizens. Those societies that revere and honor those who have gone before them will advance more quickly and with more honor.

"It pains me to see young people missing life's lessons and the wisdom they could learn through neglect of their elders. People who fail to hear these lessons from those who have gone before will eventually learn the same lessons, but at a much higher price and in a much harder way. It's true. We all pay for our education. Lessons not gained from the wisdom of the elders will undoubtedly come at a much higher price to one's own life and the life of the kingdom.

"Many people ask me how I would live my life differently if I had it to do over again. This presumes that I could live again as a young man but have the wisdom of an old man. This paradox simply does not exist in the real world. If I were a young man again, I would have my entire life before me, but I would have to learn the lessons and gain the wisdom that the years have given me.

"Life is the greatest teacher and the ultimate purveyor of wisdom. Therefore, those who have lived life should be given a platform to share their experiences and the wisdom that those experiences have brought to them."

The elderly gentleman nodded to the king, turned, and shuffled back up the aisle that led out of the Throne Room.

The king felt both excitement and frustration at the same time. He was excited about the wisdom that the eldest man in the kingdom had shared that day. He was frustrated that the simple statement of the Wisdom of the Ages he had sought so diligently still eluded him.

CHAPTER TWENTY

THE WISDOM
OF THE AGES

—ɱ—

Seek wisdom always.

HE KING WAS UNABLE TO EAT HIS DINNER. He pushed away from his table and marched to the highest point in the castle. Once there, he began pacing back and forth on the parapet as the sun set and the last glow of the day faded away. He did not enjoy the beauty of the setting sun as he had on the evening when the scientist had spoken of the marvels of nature. He continued to pace back and forth, far into the night.

He thought of each of the citizens who had shared their life's experiences and the wisdom they had discovered in them. Each of the thoughts that they had shared had been profound and significant, but still, the king was unable to distill this collective wisdom into the Wisdom of the Ages—that one universal and enduring truth that he sought as a tribute to his reign as king.

Finally, he retired to his private chambers and spent a sleepless night tossing and turning in his bed. As dawn broke, the king gave up on any attempt at sleep as he rose for the day.

A pending sense of dread built in his spirit with each tick of the clock. He knew he was expected to make the proclamation of the Wisdom of the Ages in the Throne Room later that morning.

The king's valet entered the private chambers and bowed as a greeting to the king.

He asked, "Your Majesty, what may I bring you for your breakfast this morning?"

The king replied, "I fear that I would not be able to eat anything as my anxiety about this day before us weighs heavy upon me."

The valet was very concerned, as the king had also failed to eat his dinner the night before.

"Your Highness," he asked, "is there anything that I, as your humble servant, may do to be of assistance in this matter?"

The king shook his head slowly and replied, "Not unless the Wisdom of the Ages was revealed to you during the night."

The valet said meekly, "I fear that it was not. What are you going to do?"

The king began pacing back and forth as he replied, "My honor and integrity as a leader dictates that I can only do one thing, and that is to go before the people and tell them that the Wisdom of the Ages I have sought for these many days has not been revealed to me. Therefore, we will not have a proclamation of the Wisdom of the Ages as a tribute to our people and my reign as their king."

The king delayed as long as possible, but finally it was obvious to him that he must go before the people and admit defeat. He entered the Throne Room through his private entrance, climbed the steps of the dais, and approached his throne. All of the nobility and wise men were struck by the king's haggard appearance. It was obvious he had not slept well.

As the king sat upon his throne, he contemplated how best to explain his failure in the quest for the Wisdom of the Ages. As he prepared to speak, he noticed from the corner of his eye a small form scurrying among the shadows behind the gallery where the nobility were seated.

The king spoke to the doorman nearest the back of the gallery calling, "Who goes there in the shadows? Who dares to interrupt the proceedings of the king within the Royal Throne Room? Bring that person before me."

After a moment while the guards searched the area where the sounds were heard, the doorman and two of the royal guards emerged from behind the gallery and approached the bottom step of the dais leading to the throne. Between the guards was a small girl. She thrashed about and struggled to free herself, but the guards were too strong. She stopped her fight, and her eyes grew very wide, as she found herself looking upon the king, sitting on his throne.

The king stared down at her from under his bushy eyebrows and asked, "Who might you be, and how did you get into the Throne Room of the palace?"

The wisp of a girl, maybe ten or eleven years old, replied in a timid voice, "I am just a little girl. I am very, very sorry for disturbing you, Your Highness. I know I shouldn't have done it, but I came into the palace with the crowds when everyone was pushing through the main gate. My grandma told me to stay close, but I got too curious to know where everyone was going."

"So I know how you entered the palace, which is not a crime," the king said to her. "But how did you find your way to my Throne Room, which is a crime?"

The girl gaped at him in wide-eyed terror. The king smiled at her, and with a gulp she mustered her courage to continue.

"When I was in the courtyard, Your Highness, I saw the most beautiful doorway I've ever seen in my life. Big and tall with the shiniest gold you've ever seen all over it. When I saw an old man go into it, I just followed right behind him. When I got inside, I've just been hiding so as to not bother anyone."

"You followed an old man, eh?" the king asked.

"Yes sir. And he looked very nice, he did."

"Would that door happen to be right over there to my left side?" the king asked, pointing to his private entrance.

"Yes sir."

"Well, it seems, young lady, that the old man you followed in was me. For only the king is allowed to enter that door. And last I heard, I am still the king."

Her eyes were dark and wide. The Throne Room was absolutely silent. The king, unable to contain himself any longer, suddenly burst into a fit of laughter until tears fell from his eyes. The whole assembly, with the exception of the guards whose faces were crimson with embarrassment, followed suit.

When the laughter, a welcome break to the tension that had earlier prevailed, subsided, the king inquired of the young girl, "What was so important to you this day that you would risk leaving your grandma to come into the castle and into the very Throne Room as you did?"

The dark-eyed child looked up at the king and earnestly replied, "Your Highness, when I was very young—really too young for me to remember—both of my parents were killed in a horrible accident. Since that time, I have been raised by my grandmother. She is very good to me, but she is getting too old and feeble to care for me. I only wish I was but a bit older so I could do more for her."

Tears formed at the edges of the girl's eyes. The king smiled with compassion. He wondered if he might cry himself.

"I came to the castle today, Your Majesty, because I heard you would be proclaiming the Wisdom of the Ages. The one thing that my grandmother has always taught me is to always seek wisdom. It's better than gold, she always tells me. It directs your paths. It makes for a good life.

"So, I came here today to hear wisdom, Your Highness. I don't want you to think I lied to you, but to tell the truth, even though I did think the shiny gold door was beautiful, I really went through it because I guessed that this is where you would make your announcement. I wanted to hear the Wisdom of the Ages from your own lips."

The king smiled and said, "So your grandma has told you to always seek wisdom; that it's more valuable than gold. But how will you recognize wisdom even if you do find it? And what sort of wisdom does such a young lady as yourself hope to receive to help you live your life?"

The young girl did not answer at first. Then she slowly reached into her pocket and pulled out a very old and tarnished medallion. She spoke slowly. "My grandmother gave me this and told me it has been passed down through many generations of our family. She said that the inscription on the medallion tells of true wisdom. But the words are in an old language that my family spoke hundreds of years ago, and I've never found anyone who can read it. Not even when I took it to the library."

From the front row of the gallery, the eldest wise man stood and spoke. "Your highness, may I approach?" The king looked up and beckoned his old friend and advisor to come forward.

The old wise man reached out his hand, and the young girl lovingly placed the ancient medallion in his hand. He gazed at it for several moments and positioned it to catch as much light from the stained glass windows as possible. He slowly began to read from the medallion.

"Wisdom is the daily bread of life. It is only good for one person for one day at a time. The fool will not seek wisdom, because he feels he already has it; the wise will always seek additional wisdom, because he knows he does not. Wisdom is not in the having. Wisdom is in the seeking. Always seek wisdom, and ye shall have it."

The king leapt to his feet and exclaimed, "Let it be written that this day, we have all heard wisdom. Yea, verily I say unto you, we have heard the Wisdom of the Ages. For now, we know that wisdom cannot be captured once-and-for-all, but is available to anyone and everyone who will seek it. The Wisdom of the Ages is to always seek wisdom, and it will guide you to even more wisdom. With wisdom, your life will be a gift to those around you and the world for generations to come. Wisdom is truth, and in the end, truth will find the light of day and speak for itself."

A great cheer went up in the Throne Room that reverberated throughout the castle and across the kingdom.

The king announced a holiday and a celebration through-out the land. The young girl and her grandmother were moved into the castle and lived there as special guests—and advisors—to the king.

The people of this blessed kingdom went forth seeking wisdom and sharing it with one another. They lived in peace and prosperity from generation to generation.

And their wisdom is available to us all, even to this day.

A Note from The Author

ISN'T IT AMAZING the myriad facets of wisdom that are presented to us each day? We have an opportunity to gain wisdom with every encounter, with every situation, with every challenge. The greatest journey we could ever take is the road to wisdom. It is not a destination that is reached overnight. As a matter of fact, it is a road we must discipline ourselves to remain on throughout our lives. The road to wisdom never ends.

The wisest man ever to live, according to scripture, was King Solomon. He walked the road toward wisdom, and left us many of his insights to encourage us in our journey. He encouraged subjects—as well as us today—to search for wisdom as we would for lost money or hidden treasure.

Solomon also made it clear that the beginning of this pursuit of wisdom is the fear of, or submission to, God. A proper relationship with God is essential if we are to obtain and apply wisdom in our lives.

King Solomon was not always wise. When he found himself at the helm of an eroding kingdom, facing enemies on all sides—including within his own country—he submitted himself to God, the king asking the King for help. When God asked Solomon to ask for anything, he pleaded with God for wisdom. Solomon considered wisdom a greater treasure than silver or gold. Soon he was given an opportunity to apply this wisdom.

Some time later, two prostitutes came to the king to have an argument settled. "Please, my lord," one of them began, "this woman and

I live in the same house. I gave birth to a baby while she was with me in the house. Three days later, she also had a baby. We were alone; there were only two of us in the house. But her baby died during the night when she rolled over on it. Then she got up in the night and took my son from beside me while I was asleep. She laid her dead child in my arms and took mine to sleep beside her. And in the morning when I tried to nurse my son, he was dead! But when I looked more closely in the morning light, I saw that it wasn't my son at all."

Then the other woman interrupted, "It certainly was your son, and the living child is mine."

"No," the first woman said, "the dead one is yours, and the living one is mine." And so they argued back and forth before the king.

Then the king said, "Let's get the facts straight. Both of you claim the living child is yours, and each says that the dead child belongs to the other. All right, bring me a sword." So a sword was brought to the king. Then he said, "Cut the living child in two and give half to each of these women!"

Then the woman who really was the mother of the living child, and who loved him very much, cried out, "Oh no, my lord! Give her the child—please do not kill him!"

But the other woman said, "All right, he will be neither yours nor mine; divide him between us!"

Then the king said, "Do not kill him, but give the baby to the woman who wants him to live, for she is his mother!"

Word of the king's decision spread quickly throughout all Israel, and the people were awed as they realized the great wisdom God had given him to render decisions with justice. (1 Kings 3:16-28)

You may never have to hold a sword above a child, but your decisions carry just as much weight. Starting today, make the pursuit of wisdom your life's journey.

Today's the day!

ABOUT THE AUTHOR

Jim Stovall is a highly sought-after motivational speaker. Despite failing eyesight in his teens years that led to blindness, Jim Stovall has been a national champion Olympic weight lifter, a successful investment broker, and an entrepreneur. He is the cofounder and president of the Narrative Television Network, which makes  movies and television accessible for America's 13 million blind and visually impaired people and their families. Although NTN was originally designed for the blind and visually impaired, more than 60 percent of its nationwide audience is made up of fully sighted people who simply enjoy the programming. The network's programming is also available free of charge, 24 hours a day, via the Internet at www.NarrativeTV.com.

Stovall hosts the network's talk show, *NTN Showcase*. His guests have included Katharine Hepburn, Jack Lemmon, Carol Channing, Steve Allen, and Eddie Albert, as well as many others. The Narrative Television Network has received an Emmy Award and an International Film and Video Award among its many industry honors. NTN has grown to include more than 1,200 cable systems and broadcast stations, reaching more than 35 million homes in the United States, and is shown in 11 foreign countries.

Stovall joined the ranks of Walt Disney, Orson Welles, and four U.S. presidents when he was selected as one of the Ten Outstanding Young Americans by the U.S. Junior Chamber of Commerce in 1994. He has appeared on Good Morning America and CNN, and has been featured in *Reader's Digest*, *TV Guide*, and *Time* magazines. He is the author of previous books titled *You Don't Have To Be Blind To See*, *Success Secrets of Super Achievers*, *The Way I See The World*, and *The Ultimate Gift*. The President's Committee on Equal Opportunity selected Stovall as the 1997 Entrepreneur of the Year.

In June 2000, Stovall joined notables such as President Jimmy Carter, Nancy Reagan, and Mother Teresa when he received the International Humanitarian Award.

Additional copies of this book and other
titles from RiverOak Publishing
are available from your local bookstore.

Also look for *The Ultimate Gift* by Jim Stovall.

If you have enjoyed this book,
or if it has impacted your life,
we would like to hear from you.

Please contact us at:

RiverOak Publishing
An Imprint of Cook Communications Ministries
Department E
4050 Lee Vance View
Colorado Springs, Colorado 80918

www.cookministries.com